Ursula Runde

ENGLISCH ganz leicht ZUM AUFFRISCHEN

Begleitheft

Max Hueber Verlag

Dieses Werk folgt der seit dem 1. August 1998 gültigen Rechtschreibreform.

€ 3. 2. 1. | Die letzten Ziffern
2006 05 04 03 02 | bezeichnen Zahl und Jahr des Druckes.
Alle Drucke dieser Auflage können, da unverändert,
nebeneinander benutzt werden.
1. Auflage

Titel der deutschen Originalausgabe: Hueber-Selbstlernkurs Englisch für Fortgeschrittene,

Umschlaggestaltung: Atelier Kontraste, München
Druck und Bindung: Friedrich Pustet, Regensburg
Printed in Germany
ISBN 3-19-002851-6 (Package)
2.2851 (Begleitheft)

Inhalt

1 Weekend plans

Wegweiser

Dieser Wegweiser gibt Ihnen eine kurze Übersicht über die jeweilige *Unit.* Haken Sie jeden Abschnitt ab, nachdem Sie ihn durchgearbeitet haben.

	Dialog 1 Hören Sie sich den Dialog bei geschlossenem Buch an.
	Hören Sie sich den Dialog bei geöffnetem Buch an (wenn nötig, mehrmals).
	Studieren Sie Vokabeln und Erklärungen zu Dialog 1.
	Bearbeiten Sie die zum Dialog gehörenden Übungen.
	Dialog 2 Hören Sie sich den Dialog bei geschlossenem Buch an.
	Hören Sie sich den Dialog bei geöffnetem Buch an (wenn nötig, mehrmals).
	Studieren Sie Vokabeln und Erklärungen zu Dialog 2.
	Bearbeiten Sie die zum Dialog gehörenden Übungen.
	Dialog 3 Hören Sie sich den Dialog bei geschlossenem Buch an.
	Hören Sie sich den Dialog bei geöffnetem Buch an (wenn nötig, mehrmals).
	Studieren Sie Vokabeln und Erklärungen zu Dialog 3.
	Bearbeiten Sie die zum Dialog gehörenden Übungen.
	Prägen Sie sich die *Wichtigen Wörter und Ausdrücke* ein.
	Arbeiten Sie die *Grammatik* durch und bearbeiten Sie die Übungen.
	Bearbeiten Sie die *Leseübungen.*
	Nun folgen die *Radioauszüge* mit den dazugehörigen *Übungen.*
	Sprechen Sie selbst.
	Hören Sie sich alle Dialoge und Radiotexte noch einmal ohne Buch an.

Lösungen

Dialog 1

Übung 1: a. Windsor; b. Stratford-on-Avon; c. Stonehenge; d. Kew Gardens; e. Cambridge; f. Greenwich.

Übung 2: a. Cambridge; b. Greenwich; c. Kew Gardens; d. Stonehenge; e. Stratford-on-Avon; f. Windsor.

Dialog 2

Übung 4: Theatre visit, ballet, conversation, Spanish evening.

Übung 5: chance ... dancing ... performance ... rehearsal ... backstage; tickets.

Übung 6: TUESDAY AUGUST 2nd: New students' party; THURSDAY AUGUST 4th: Around London Tour; FRIDAY AUGUST 5th: Conversation Exchange; SATURDAY AUGUST 6th: Excursion to Cambridge.

Dialog 3

Übung 8: a./1; b./4; c./2; d./3.

Übung 9: a. ... being indoors all the time; b. Assuming ...; c. ... cheap fares on the tube ...; d. ... play it by ear ...

Grammatik

Übung 1: a. It can't be possible! b. Can you ride? c. I'll come as soon as I can. d. Do your homework. Your sister can help you. e. My father can't see well. f. She can speak French very well.

Übung 2: a. could; b. could; c. managed to; d. managed to; e. could; f. managed to.

Leseübungen

Übung 1: a. drei; b. einen Tag; c. einen Monat; d. £35; e. nein; f. man muss sich an die Orte halten, die *British Rail* ausgewählt hat; g. nein – auch in Europa und Nordamerika.

Übung 2: b. Southend; c. Richmond; d. Windsor; e. Rochester; f. Hampton Court; g. St. Albans.

Radioübungen

Übung 1, Text

Jonathan Pearce (reporter): Sports news, starting with athletics. And Sussex's international middle distance runner Sue Morley will miss out on the chance to meet South African born Zola Budd at Crawley this weekend. The Brighton runner is training in Asateas, Portugal, and won't be back in time to run against Zola at the opening meeting of the new three hundred thousand pound Crawley athletics arena. Miss Budd will use the fifteen hundred metre run as another step in her bid to earn British Olympic selection. Local runners have a mixed reaction to her taking part. Crawley's Debbie Peel says it could open the way to more foreign runners being given British citizenship but Brighton and Hove team manager Debbie Thomas says her appearance can only benefit the sports.

Debbie Thomas: I hope it's going to be a big attraction. In fact the meeting on Saturday is to mark the opening of a new Crawley track so I think it'll be a good boost to the Crawley club and also to anybody that's going along to watch.

Übung 1, Lösung: a./F; b./F; c./T; d./T; e./T; f./F.

Übung 2 und 3, Text

Stuart MacIntosh: Now the weather forecast. The afternoon will be dry and it'll stay mostly sunny. Temperatures will peak at 13 degrees centigrade except along the coast where the light to moderate force 2 to 4 southerly breezes restrict temperatures to 11 degrees centigrade. Overnight it's going to stay dry with clear spells, temperatures falling to around 2 degrees centigrade resulting in ground frost and patchy mist or fog over inland valleys. Winds will remain light and mainly southerly, and the outlook for tomorrow, dry and bright.

Übung 2, Lösung: breeze – breezy; frost – frosty; fog – foggy; drizzle – drizzly; rain – rainy; shower – showery; cloud – cloudy.

Übung 3: a./2; b./2; c./2; d./1; e./3; f./2.

2 Non-stop to Florida

Wegweiser

	Dialog 1 Hören Sie sich den Dialog bei geschlossenem Buch an.
	Hören Sie sich den Dialog bei geöffnetem Buch an, sooft Sie wollen.
	Studieren Sie Vokabeln und Erklärungen zu Dialog 1.
	Bearbeiten Sie die zum Dialog gehörenden Übungen.
	Dialog 2 Hören Sie sich den Dialog bei geschlossenem Buch an.
	Hören Sie sich den Dialog bei geöffnetem Buch an, sooft Sie wollen.
	Studieren Sie Vokabeln und Erklärungen zu Dialog 2.
	Bearbeiten Sie die zum Dialog gehörenden Übungen.
	Dialog 3 Hören Sie sich den Dialog bei geschlossenem Buch an.
	Hören Sie sich den Dialog bei geöffnetem Buch an, sooft Sie wollen.
	Studieren Sie Vokabeln und Erklärungen zu Dialog 3.
	Bearbeiten Sie die zum Dialog gehörenden Übungen.
	Dialog 4 Hören Sie sich den Dialog bei geschlossenem Buch an.
	Hören Sie sich den Dialog bei geöffnetem Buch an, sooft Sie wollen.
	Studieren Sie Vokabeln und Erklärungen zu Dialog 4.
	Bearbeiten Sie die zum Dialog gehörenden Übungen.
	Prägen Sie sich die *Wichtigen Wörter und Ausdrücke* ein.
	Arbeiten Sie die *Grammatik* durch und bearbeiten Sie die Übungen.
	Bearbeiten Sie die *Leseübungen*.

	Nun folgen die *Radioauszüge* mit den dazugehörigen Übungen.
	Sprechen Sie selbst.
	Hören Sie sich alle CD-Texte noch einmal ohne Buch an.

Lösungen

Dialog 1

Übung 1: Reihenfolge: e., a., c., g., f., d., b.

Übung 2: a./2, b./3, c./1, d./3, e./1.

Dialog 2

Übung 4: b./VII, c./II, d./VI, e./III, f./V, g./I.

Übung 5: passports, swimming costumes, a tent, blankets, sleeping bags, suntan lotion, a guide to camp sites, sunglasses.

Dialog 3

Übung 7: . . . windsurf . . . sun-tan . . . boom . . . water . . . language.

Übung 8: a./3, b./1, c./3, d./2.

Dialog 4

Übung 10: a./3, 4; b./2; c./3, 4; d./3; e./3.

Übung 11: a. CONCERT; b. NEWS; c. CELEBRATE; d. SERIES; e. PROMOTE; f. LISTENERS; g. DRAMA; h. RADIO; i. CONTROLLER; j. CHRISTMAS; k. ENJOY; l. FRIENDS; m. ORCHESTRA = ENTERTAINMENT.

Grammatik

Übung 1: be/was, were; bring/brought; buy/bought; catch/caught; do/did; eat/ate; get/got; go/went; see/saw; put/put; let/let; talk/talked; speak/spoke; meet/met; want/wanted; can/could; have/had; know/knew.

Übung 2: a. happened; b. was looking, saw; c. was hurrying, were walking; d. tried, was; e. turned, saw; f. was she smiling? g. I did not know.

Leseübungen

Übung 1: a./I, b./V, c./IV, d./III, e./II.

Übung 2: b. 26th Dec.; c. 25th Dec.; d. 24th Dec.; e. 25th Dec.; f. 26th Dec.; g. 25th Dec.; h. 24th Dec.; i. 25th Dec.; j. 25th Dec.; k. 26th Dec.

Radioübungen

Übung 1, Text

Chris Reilly: Keeping children out of trouble and danger during holidays is always a problem for parents. Neil Halley works in the amenities and tourist office at Worthing Council. He says the most important thing when away with the kids is to keep them busy.

Neil Halley: Children need to be occupied, this is the important thing. Obviously parents have got to choose a resort in which children can enjoy themselves. At Worthing we have Brookland's Pleasure Park. There is the swimming pools and the sea and the seashore. There are also pitch and putt courses, putting courses, and many other things similar to that.

Reilly: What do you find that children need and like most?

Neil Halley: I think being occupied and the fact that they are at the seaside, the sea is always an attraction. All we hope is that when parents do bring children that they do look after them and keep an eye on them. That's the important thing.

Übung 1, Lösung: b. liegt zwischen Land und Meer; c. öffentliche (Freizeit)einrichtungen; d. Gemeinderat; e. Kinder auf Trab halten; f. Erholungsort.

Übung 2, Text

I

Travel On Man: Fly Gatwick to New York for only £99. That's right, £99. With the new Virgin Atlantic Airways. Tickets are now available from Travel On in Hove. Call Travel On now on Brighton 731661. That's 731661. Fly Gatwick to New York for only £99. Phone Travel On on Brighton 731661.

II

(Phone rings)
Mum: Hello.
Jenny: Hello Mum, it's Jenny.
Mum: Oh!
Jenny: We're having a fabulous holiday here in Florida.
Mum: But Jenny –
Jenny: We flew to Tampa with Arrow Air. It's the only non-stop service from London, and they've got the lowest fares.
Mum: Oh really?
Jenny: They looked after us beautifully, especially the kids. It was a really comfortable flight.
Mum: Is ...?
Jenny: The weather's fantastic and there's masses to do. We've been to Walt Disney World and Sea World and had some smashing days on the beach and John's played loads of golf.
Mum: Who?
Jenny: We flew with Arrow Air! The only non-stop service to Tampa!
Arrow Air Man: Non-stop Florida by Arrow Air. See your travel agent or call Gatwick 548181. That's Gatwick 548181, Arrow Air. You just can't stop people talking about us.

Übung 2, Lösung: a. Travel On; b. Travel On; c. Arrow Air; d. Travel On; e. Arrow Air; f. Travel On; g. Arrow Air; h. Travel On; i. Arrow Air.

3 What time will you be free?

Wegweiser

	Dialog 1 Hören Sie sich den Dialog bei geschlossenem Buch an.
	Hören Sie sich den Dialog beliebig oft bei geöffnetem Buch an.
	Arbeiten Sie die Vokabeln und Erklärungen durch.
	Machen Sie die zum Dialog gehörenden Übungen.
	Dialog 2 Hören Sie sich den Dialog bei geschlossenem Buch an.
	Hören Sie sich den Dialog bei geöffnetem Buch an.
	Studieren Sie Vokabeln und Erklärungen zu Dialog 2.

	Bearbeiten Sie die zum Dialog gehörenden Übungen.
	Dialog 3 Hören Sie sich den Dialog bei geschlossenem Buch an.
	Hören Sie sich den Dialog bei geöffnetem Buch an.
	Studieren Sie Vokabeln und Erklärungen zu Dialog 3.
	Bearbeiten Sie die zum Dialog gehörenden Übungen.
	Dialog 4 Hören Sie sich den Dialog bei geschlossenem Buch an.
	Hören Sie sich den Dialog bei geöffnetem Buch an.
	Studieren Sie Vokabeln und Erklärungen zu Dialog 4.
	Bearbeiten Sie die zum Dialog gehörenden Übungen.
	Prägen Sie sich die *Wichtigen Wörter und Ausdrücke* ein.
	Bearbeiten Sie die *Leseübungen* (diesmal *vor* der Grammatik!)
	Studieren Sie die *Grammatik* und machen Sie die Übungen dazu.
	Hören Sie sich die *Radioauszüge* an und machen Sie die Übungen.
	Sprechen Sie selbst.
	Hören Sie sich alle Dialoge und Radiotexte noch einmal ohne Buch an.

Lösungen

Dialog 1

Übung 1: a./F; b./F; c./T; d./T; e./T; f./F; g./T; h./T; i./T; j./F.

Übung 2: Zeichnung 1 = a., Zeichnung 2 = d., Zeichnung 3 = e., Zeichnung 4 = b., Zeichnung 5 = c.

Dialog 2

Übung 4: Die richtige Version ist b.

Übung 5: a. How do you fancy popping; b. as you might expect; c. I really would love to (go); d. I've often intended going; e. let's do it today; f. That suits me fine; g. Right.

Dialog 3

Übung 7: I/b., II/c., III/e., IV/a., V/d.

Übung 8: ... usually ... invariably ... about ... attacked ... manner ... good fight ... run-around ... ready ... amount ... telephone.

Dialog 4

Übung 10: a. Nein. b. Weil es in London ein chinesisches Viertel *(Chinatown)* gibt. c. Sehr einfach. d. Als sie bei einer englischen Familie wohnte. e. Nein, nur einige.

Übung 11: problems ... food ... meals ... breakfast ... marvellous ... cooks ... variety ... lunch.

Leseübungen

Übung 1: a./2.; b./3.; c./2.; d./3.; e./1.; f./2.

Übung 2: a. At six a. m. b. When she has only a small part in a film or play. c. Not completely, she still occasionally gets it. d. No, she doesn't. e. She used to raid the fridge and eat everything she could lay her hands on. f. No, she doesn't. g. In the bath.

Grammatik

Übung 1: a. Every morning I would get up at seven. b. I would have a shower and brush my teeth. c. I wouldn't have breakfast, just a cup of tea. d. I used to be always just in time at the station. e. I used to read the newspaper on my way to work. f. I sometimes used to fall asleep and would miss my stop.

Übung 2: a. I used to drink mineral water, but now I don't. b. I used to watch much television, but now I prefer going to the cinema. c. I used to be afraid of flying, but now I enjoy it. d. I didn't use to like strong coffee, but now I love it.

Radioübungen

Übung 1, Text

Brighton Poly language course woman: Aimeriez-vous parler français aussi bien que cela? *(Würden Sie auch gerne so gut Französisch sprechen?)*
Man: At Brighton Polytechnic Language Centre we have courses in a variety of languages and at all levels, from beginner to diploma standard. Our courses are structured to make the best use of your time whether you're on a part time or intensive course. We also have residential courses available. So whether it's a feeling for French, a grounding in Greek, a gentle introduction to German, a smattering of Spanish, an inkling of Italian or a reminder of Russian, call the Language Centre at Brighton Polytechnic. Telephone Brighton 606 622. But do it soon.

Übung 1, Lösung: language ... beginners' ... intensive ... residential ... variety ... Greek, Russian ... phone.

Übung 2, Text

Chris Copsey: In 1966 the age of steam and latterly diesel came to an end after just over a hundred years of transportation and now Beechings cover the area. Peter calling from Henfield. Hello Peter.
Peter: Hello.
Chris Copsey: The answer is?
Peter: Well I reckon it's Henfield.
Chris Copsey: It is Henfield. Well done. Some clues gave it away. Which was the actual clue that gave it away?
Peter: Well there's – the railway was axed in 66 of course.
Chris Copsey: That's right.
Peter: And the old railway station, the –
Chris Copsey: It's now –
Peter: Beechings Estate there now.
Chris Copsey: That's right, the actual station buildings are called Beechings Housing Estate, the railway line now used as a bridle way.

Übung 2, Lösung: a., b. und e. wurden erwähnt.

4 Take the Awayday Ticket!

Wegweiser

	Dialog 1 Hören Sie sich den Dialog bei geschlossenem Buch an.
	Hören Sie sich den Dialog beliebig oft bei geöffnetem Buch an.
	Studieren Sie die Vokabeln und Erklärungen.
	Bearbeiten Sie die zum Dialog gehörenden Übungen.
	Dialog 2 Hören Sie sich den Dialog bei geschlossenem Buch an.
	Hören Sie sich den Dialog bei geöffnetem Buch an.
	Studieren Sie Vokabeln und Erklärungen zu Dialog 2.
	Bearbeiten Sie die zum Dialog gehörenden Übungen.
	Dialog 3 Hören Sie sich den Dialog bei geschlossenem Buch an.
	Hören Sie sich den Dialog bei geöffnetem Buch an.
	Studieren Sie Vokabeln und Erklärungen zu Dialog 3.
	Bearbeiten Sie die zum Dialog gehörenden Übungen.
	Dialog 4 Hören Sie sich den Dialog bei geschlossenem Buch an.
	Hören Sie sich den Dialog bei geöffnetem Buch an.
	Studieren Sie Vokabeln und Erklärungen zu Dialog 4.
	Bearbeiten Sie die zum Dialog gehörenden Übungen.
	Prägen Sie sich die *Wichtigen Wörter und Ausdrücke* ein.
	Arbeiten Sie die *Grammatik* durch und bearbeiten Sie die Übungen.
	Bearbeiten Sie die *Leseübungen*.

	Nun folgen die *Radioauszüge* mit den dazugehörigen Übungen.
	Sprechen Sie selbst.
	Hören Sie sich alle CD-Texte noch einmal ohne Buch an.

Lösungen

Dialog 1

Übung 1: a. Ford Escort; b. hatchback; c. 3; d. £19.50; e. £2.75.

Übung 2: a./V, b./IV, c./III, d./I, e./II.

Dialog 2

Übung 4: a./3, b./2, c./2, d./3, e./1.

Übung 5: a. coming over; b. possibilities; c. which allows them; d. farther afield; e. cheap price.

Dialog 3

Übung 7: a./2, b./2, c./3, d./3, e./3.

Übung 8: 10.55 LH 069/Mon–Fri; 18.10 LH 070/Sun.

Dialog 4

Übung 10: a. = 2, b. = 4, c. = 3, d. = 1.

Übung 11: a. den Zug um 9.09 h; b. den Zug um 9.35 h; c. ungefähr um 9.30 h; d. um 19 h; e. 3 (mindestens).

Grammatik

Übung 1: a. Don't put it off any longer. b. At which station do we have to get off? c. The thieves made off with a lot of money. d. I feel very let down. e. Don't get on this bus!

Übung 2: a. six pound ninety-nine; b. four pound seven ounces; c. three point fifty-six kilometres; d. seven elevenths; e. one and a third.

Leseübungen

Übung 1: a. Firma C, b. Firma A, c. Firma B, d. Firma D, e. Firma B, f. Firma D, g. Firma D.

Übung 2: a. Heathrow; b. Luton; c. Luton; d. Gatwick; e. Heathrow; f. Gatwick; g. Luton.

Radioübungen

Übung 1 und 2: Text

John Mann: Southern Sound Radio, it's 10 minutes to 5. If you're taking a train this evening or meeting someone at the station, you'll be pleased to know that trains in Sussex are running smoothly. It's not such a happy picture on the roads though. There are long queues of traffic on the A 23 north of Brighton on the Pyecombe fork and there's resurfacing work all week where the A 273 comes in. There's only one lane open in both directions so you may be delayed by up to 20 minutes; and allow extra time for your journey if you're going along this stretch. Also long hold-ups on the A 27 at Fishbourne, where you'll find temporary traffic lights, and also on the A 27 in Brighton. Elsewhere there are several sets of road-works on the A 259 at Littlehampton, Climping, and at Rustington. It's a good evening if you're travelling by bus, plane of ferry, all services are operating normally and that's it from Travelwise.

Übung 1, Lösung:

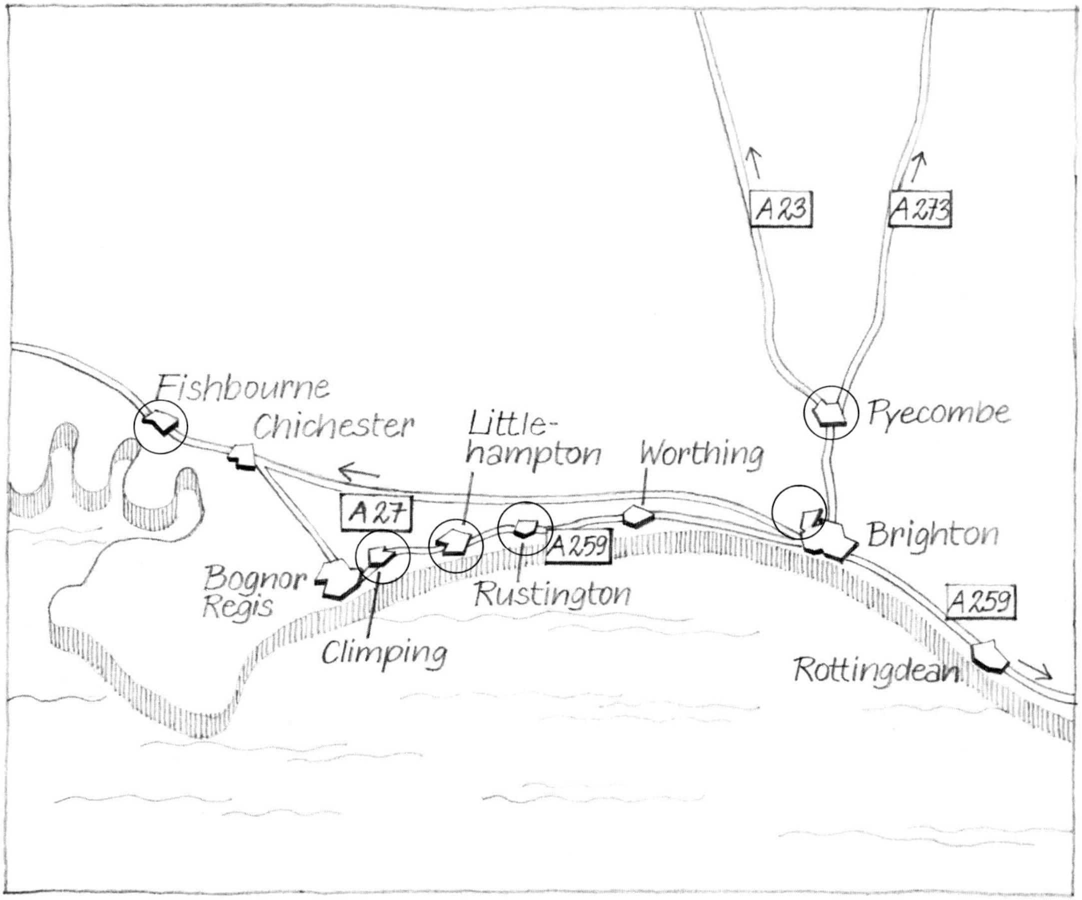

Übung 2, Lösung: Kästchen a. und c.

5 Would you like a starter?

Wegweiser

	Dialog 1 Hören Sie sich den Dialog zunächst bei geschlossenem Buch an.
	Hören Sie sich den Dialog mehrmals bei geöffnetem Buch an.
	Studieren Sie die Vokabeln und Erklärungen.
	Bearbeiten Sie die zum Dialog gehörenden Übungen.
	Dialog 2 Hören Sie sich den Dialog bei geschlossenem Buch an.
	Hören Sie sich den Dialog bei geöffnetem Buch an (wenn nötig, mehrmals).
	Studieren Sie Vokabeln und Erklärungen zu Dialog 2.
	Bearbeiten Sie die zum Dialog gehörenden Übungen.
	Dialog 3 Hören Sie sich den Dialog bei geschlossenem Buch an.
	Hören Sie sich den Dialog bei geöffnetem Buch an (wenn nötig, mehrmals).
	Studieren Sie Vokabeln und Erklärungen zu Dialog 3.
	Bearbeiten Sie die zum Dialog gehörenden Übungen.
	Dialog 4 Hören Sie sich den Dialog bei geschlossenem Buch an.
	Hören Sie sich den Dialog bei geöffnetem Buch an (wenn nötig, mehrmals).
	Studieren Sie Vokabeln und Erklärungen zu Dialog 4.
	Bearbeiten Sie die zum Dialog gehörenden Übungen.
	Prägen Sie sich die *Wichtigen Wörter und Ausdrücke* ein.
	Arbeiten Sie die *Grammatik* durch und bearbeiten Sie die Übungen.
	Bearbeiten Sie die *Leseübung* (diesmal nur eine).

	Nun folgen im *Radioabschnitt* 3 Anzeigen mit den dazugehörigen *Übungen.*
	Sprechen Sie selbst.
	Hören Sie sich alle CD-Texte noch einmal ohne Buch an.

Lösungen

Dialog 1

Übung 1: Vorspeise: French onion soup, Hauptspeise: Lamb Satay, Wein: Muscadet.

Übung 2: b./I, c./V, d./III, e./II.

Dialog 2

Übung 4: a./1, b./3, c./3, d./2, e./1.

Übung 5:

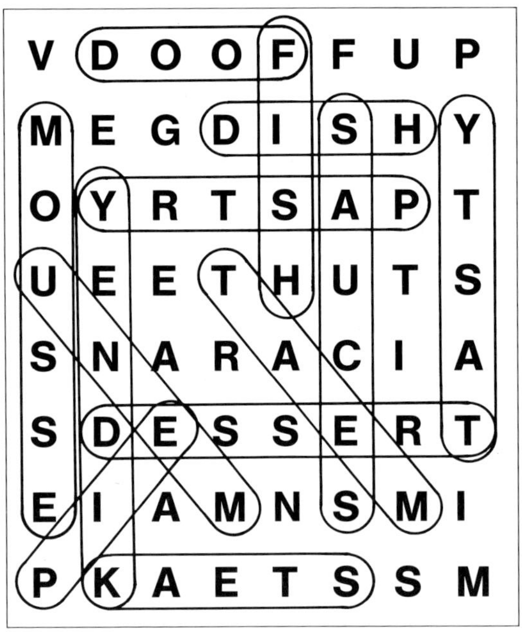

Dialog 3

Übung 7: b., e., f.

Übung 8: a. No; b. No; c. Yes; d. No; e. No; f. Yes.

Dialog 4

Übung 10: Positiv: superb, jolly well, helpful. Negativ: despicable, atrocious, rude, unhygienic, really bad.

Übung 11: Dear Sir, a few months ago one could still eat really well at your restaurant. But now? I wanted to order something last night, but I simply couldn't get any service. When the waitress finally came, she was very rude. And the food was cold and not well cooked. And (all) that at a price of £12.50. It's a scandal!

Grammatik

Übung 1: a. We haven't got any fresh fruit today. b. We haven't got any Algerian wine. c. There aren't any Chinese dishes on the menu. d. There aren't any flowers on the table. e. There aren't any special knives and forks for the fish dishes.

Übung 2: a. We have no fresh fruit today. b. We have no Algerian wine. c. There are no Chinese dishes on the menu. d. There are no flowers on the table. e. There are no special knives and forks for the fish dishes.

Leseübung

Jeweils von oben nach unten: d, b, f, c, e, a, h, g.

Radioübungen

Übung 1 und 2, Text

I

Man: Morning, darling. Last night was wonderful.
Woman: Was rather rich and fruity, wasn't it?
Man: Mm. The best you've done in ages. Hey, what was so different?

Woman: The fruit! I got it from that smashing greengrocery at the Food Warehouse. Made all the difference to the summer pudding. Firm and fresh and very fruity.
Man 2: The Food Warehouse. South side of Hove station, open 8 a. m. to 8 p. m. Monday to Saturday with free parking. It's where less frills mean lower bills.

II

There's a new opening for traders in Brighton. Linfood Cash and Carry is coming to town and the doors are open to the best trade prices around on Sunday the 15th of April at 9 a. m. If you're in the food business, whether for retailing or catering, it's a must.
You'll find us on the site of the old Kemptown railway station on the Freshfield Industrial Estate. Make a date for Sunday the 15th at 9 a. m. at Linfood.

III

Salesman: Are you the manager?
Manager: Yes.
Salesman: Ah, good morning. I've got some great little gimmicks for you.
Manager: No thanks.
Salesman: Look, super luminous posters. Your customers won't miss these.
Manager: No.
Salesman: Shelf wobblers – great little promotions.
Manager: No.
Salesman: Background music? D'you fancy some really –
Manager: No thanks.
Shoppers Paradise spokesman: At Shoppers Paradise there are no expensive frills, no music, no fancy displays. What we save on gimmicks we pass on to you as price cuts. You'll find all your favourite big brands like Princes, KP, Chambourcy, all you need for your weekly shopping at the lowest possible prices. So start saving money today at Shoppers Paradise, the lowest food price list in town.

Übung 1, Lösung: a. = III, b. = II, c. = I.
a. ... paradise ... price list ... favourite brands; b. cash ... 15th April ... industrial estate; c. frills ... bills ... food ... Monday.

Übung 2: a. = III, b. = II, c. = II, d. = I, e. = I.

6 Yes, I'm a jogger!

Wegweiser

	Dialog 1 Hören Sie sich den Dialog bei geschlossenem Buch an.
	Hören Sie sich den Dialog mehrmals bei geöffnetem Buch an.
	Studieren Sie die Vokabeln und Erklärungen.
	Bearbeiten Sie die zum Dialog gehörenden Übungen.
	Dialog 2 Hören Sie sich den Dialog bei geschlossenem Buch an.

	Hören Sie sich den Dialog bei geöffnetem Buch an (wenn nötig, mehrmals).
	Studieren Sie Vokabeln und Erklärungen zu Dialog 2.
	Bearbeiten Sie die zum Dialog gehörenden Übungen.
	Dialog 3 Hören Sie sich den Dialog bei geschlossenem Buch an.
	Hören Sie sich den Dialog bei geöffnetem Buch an (wenn nötig, mehrmals).
	Studieren Sie Vokabeln und Erklärungen zu Dialog 3.
	Bearbeiten Sie die zum Dialog gehörenden Übungen.
	Dialog 4 Hören Sie sich den Dialog bei geschlossenem Buch an.
	Hören Sie sich den Dialog bei geöffnetem Buch an (wenn nötig, mehrmals).
	Studieren Sie Vokabeln und Erklärungen zu Dialog 4.
	Bearbeiten Sie die zum Dialog gehörenden Übungen.
	Prägen Sie sich die *Wichtigen Wörter und Ausdrücke* ein.
	Arbeiten Sie die *Grammatik* durch und bearbeiten Sie die Übungen.
	Bearbeiten Sie die *Leseübungen.*
	Nun folgen die *Radioauszüge* mit den dazugehörigen Übungen.
	Sprechen Sie selbst.
	Hören Sie sich alle CD-Texte noch einmal ohne Buch an.

Lösungen

Dialog 1

Übung 1: a. a packet of disposable nappies; b. a bottle of sun-tan lotion; c. a packet of anti-diarrhoea tablets; d. a bottle of shampoo; e. a bar of soap; f. a bottle of anti-diarrhoea medicine; g. a tube of insect-repellent cream; h. a can of insect-repellent spray.

Übung 2: disinfectant, disposable nappies, aspirin tablets, toilet soap, shaving cream, toothpaste, aftershave lotion, sunglasses, nail scissors.

Dialog 2

Übung 4: a./2, b./1, c./3, d./3, e./2.

Übung 5: a. Ginny, b. nobody, c. her husband, d. her children, e. nobody, f. her children, g. nobody.

Dialog 3

Übung 7: a. = 1, i. = 2, e. = 3, h. = 4, f. = 5, b. = 6, g. = 7, d. = 8, c. = 9, k = 10, j. = 11.

Übung 8: b. = E, c. = A, d. = F, e. = B, f. = D.

Dialog 4

Übung 10: b, d, e, g.

Übung 11: a./2, b./1, c./2, d./1.

Grammatik

Übung 1: a. I'll answer it; b. I'll pay it; c. I'll stop it; d. I'll fix it.

Übung 2: a. Shall I get you one more glass of wine? b. You shall get a new bicycle! c. You shall not talk when I'm speaking! d. What shall we do now? e. Shall we go to the cinema or to the theatre?

Leseübungen

Übung 1: Eat more: carrots, cottage cheese, skimmed milk, dried fruit, corn oil, sunflower oil. Eat less: mince, pastries, squashes, tinned soup, lard.

Übung 2:

F	I	R	S	V	B	E
I	R	I	C	E	D	S
S	T	R	U	G	O	Y
H	I	S	A	E	P	R
A	U	T	D	T	Z	T
S	R	U	N	A	F	L
N	F	N	A	B	R	U
A	R	A	T	L	G	O
E	W	E	K	E	P	P
B	Z	P	A	S	T	A

Radioübungen

Übung 1, Text

Andrew Winter: If you've just bought a new fridge or freezer, make sure your old one is safe before you throw it out. Smash the doorcatch and remove the hinges, then there's no danger of a child getting trapped inside before you have it taken away. And while we're on the subject of appliances in the home, portable gas heaters should always have a guard on them just as if they were solid fuel or electric. Remember to keep portable gas heaters away from your furniture and make sure all the appliances and flexible tubing are in good condition. And that all the connectors are gasboard approved. Don't forget that heaters need air too so always keep your room well-ventilated. And, following on from fires, many fires in the home start at night. They can be caused by cigarettes left smouldering which eventually set fire to upholstered furniture and beds. If you have an electric blanket, make sure that you follow the manufacturer's instructions for use and maintenance. See that cigarettes are safely put out and that electrical appliances such as fires and television sets are switched off and unplugged. And close all the doors before going to bed.

Übung 1, Lösung: a./E, b./B, c./D, d./A, e./F, f./C.

Übung 2, Text

(Music) Look out for the Shape Health Studios Super Saver Voucher coming through your door. Shape are offering an incredible 50 per cent discount off the price of membership on production of your Super Saver Voucher. That's Shape Health Studios in Devonshire Place, Brighton, and the King Alfred Centre, Hove. Remember, 50 per cent off Shape Membership if you produce your Super Saver Voucher. But hurry! Offer finishes May the 7th.

Übung 2, Lösung: Shape up at Shape *Health Studios*! Yes! With the *Super* Saver *Voucher*! Incredible discount price! Hurry! *Offer* closes May 7th! 50% discount. Your own personal *saver voucher*! 50% discount membership! Shape Health Studios, Devonshire Place, Brighton, or *King Alfred Centre*, Hove.

7 Bring a bottle!

Wegweiser

	Dialog 1 Hören Sie sich den Dialog bei geschlossenem Buch an.
	Hören Sie sich den Dialog mehrmals bei geöffnetem Buch an.
	Studieren Sie die Vokabeln und Erklärungen zu dem Dialog.
	Machen Sie die zum Dialog gehörenden Übungen.
	Dialog 2 Hören Sie sich den Dialog bei geschlossenem Buch an.
	Hören Sie sich den Dialog bei geöffnetem Buch an (wenn nötig, mehrmals).
	Studieren Sie Vokabeln und Erklärungen zu Dialog 2.
	Bearbeiten Sie die zum Dialog gehörenden Übungen.
	Dialog 3 Hören Sie sich den Dialog bei geschlossenem Buch an.
	Hören Sie sich den Dialog bei geöffnetem Buch an (wenn nötig, mehrmals).
	Studieren Sie Vokabeln und Erklärungen zu Dialog 3.
	Bearbeiten Sie die zum Dialog gehörenden Übungen.
	Prägen Sie sich die *Wichtigen Wörter und Ausdrücke* ein.
	Arbeiten Sie die *Grammatik* durch und bearbeiten Sie die Übungen.
	Bearbeiten Sie die *Leseübungen.*
	Nun folgen die *Radioauszüge* mit den dazugehörigen Übungen.
	Sprechen Sie selbst.
	Hören Sie sich alle CD-Texte noch einmal ohne Buch an.

Lösungen

Dialog 1

Übung 1: a./3, b./2, c./3, d./2, e./1.

Dialog 2

Übung 4: a. Weil viele Leute herumstehen und es am besten ist, wenn sie sich selbst bedienen können. b. Weil die Autofahrer unter den Gästen nicht so viel Alkohol trinken wollen. c. Man bringt zur Party eine Flasche *(bottle)* mit. d. Sie ist billiger. e. Nicht zu laut und aufdringlich.

Übung 5: a. DANCE; b. ORDEAL; c. STRIDENT; d. PROVIDE; e. CHOICE; f. PLANNING; g. GLASS= **DRIVING**.

Dialog 3

Übung 7:

S	D	E	E	S	N	M	U
D	N	U	O	P	O	W	T
C	A	R	D	A	M	O	M
L	P	S	U	G	A	R	E
L	P	O	T	E	N	A	R
D	L	W	I	N	N	N	T
H	E	A	T	E	I	G	I
S	E	V	O	L	C	E	L

„Mulled wine"

Übung 8: a. litres; b. a lot ... a few; c. half a pound; d. an ... two.

Grammatik

Übung 1: a. If I never had a holiday, I would feel very tired. b. If you stopped working, would you be bored? c. If we learned to communicate, the world would be more peaceful. d. If he didn't eat so much, he wouldn't be so fat. e. If we were rich, we could travel a lot.

Übung 2: a./V, b./I, c./II, d./III, e./IV.

Leseübungen

Übung 1: a. 45, b. 45, c. 5, d. 20, e. 20, f. 20, g. 45, h. 45, i. 5, j. 5, k. 45, l. 20.

Übung 2: 1 = a., 2 = h., 3 = b., 4 = k., 5 = g., 6 = e., 7 = l., 8 = f., 9 = d., 10 = i., 11 = j., 12 = c.

Radioübungen

Übung 1, Text

If you're there this evening or at the weekend, try a really great pub. Like the popular Railway Tavern on Station Road, Ports Lane. It's recently been nicely done up. You'll get a warm welcome too at the Hiker's Rest on Coldean Lane, Brighton. Good food and beer and good facilities for darts, pool and bar billiards. The Britannia, Grinstead Lane, in Lancing, has similar attractions with hot and cold food and roomy and comfortable bars. All great pubs. The Railway Tavern, Ports Lane, the Hiker's Rest, Coldean Lane, Brighton, and the Britannia at Lancing. A few tips from Charrington. Let's see you soon.

Übung 1, Lösung: a./B, b./RT, c./HR, d./B, e./HR, f./HR, g./HR.

Übung 2, 3 und 4, Text

Andrew Winter: There are many books in existence about the types of wine and how you should serve them and when. But, as we all know, the various types of wine in existence are red, white or rosé and they can either be light or heavy; dry, medium and sweet; still or sparkling.

But the traditional accompaniment for soup is sherry; shellfish and fish should be accompanied by a dry white wine; rich or highly seasoned red meat and game are particularly good with a full-bodied red wine, typically a burgundy. Other red meat goes

well with lighter red wine such as Bordeaux. Now white meat can be accompanied by a light red wine or a medium dry white wine. Cheese can be eaten with red and of course that's the ideal background for any sort of port. Sweet wine, though, or champagne is usually served with puddings.
Now the temperature at which wines can taste best varies according to their type. Red wines are normally served at room temperature as are port and madeira. Champagne though should always be served cold, though not frozen; and the same applies to white wines and rosé.

Übung 2, Lösung: a. red meat; b. game; c. puddings; d. cheese, puddings; e. soup; f. fish, white meat.

Übung 3, Beispiele: d. Port goes well with cheese, and sweet wine with any sort of pudding. e. Soup should be accompanied by sherry, that's the tradition. f. Usually a white wine is served with fish dishes and white meat.

Übung 4, Lösung: b. cold, not frozen; c. cold, not frozen; d. room temperature; e. cold, not frozen; f. room temperature.

8 I like documentary programmes

Wegweiser

	Dialog 1 Hören Sie sich den Dialog bei geschlossenem Buch an.
	Hören Sie sich den Dialog bei geöffnetem Buch an (wenn nötig, mehrmals).
	Studieren Sie Vokabeln und Erklärungen zu Dialog 1.
	Bearbeiten Sie die zum Dialog gehörenden Übungen.
	Dialog 2 Hören Sie sich den Dialog bei geschlossenem Buch an.
	Hören Sie sich den Dialog bei geöffnetem Buch an (wenn nötig, mehrmals).
	Studieren Sie Vokabeln und Erklärungen zu Dialog 2.
	Bearbeiten Sie die zum Dialog gehörenden Übungen.
	Dialog 3 Hören Sie sich den Dialog bei geschlossenem Buch an.
	Hören Sie sich den Dialog bei geöffnetem Buch an (wenn nötig, mehrmals).
	Studieren Sie Vokabeln und Erklärungen zu Dialog 3.

	Bearbeiten Sie die zum Dialog gehörenden Übungen.
	Dialog 4 Hören Sie sich den Dialog bei geschlossenem Buch an.
	Hören Sie sich den Dialog bei geöffnetem Buch an (wenn nötig, mehrmals).
	Studieren Sie Vokabeln und Erklärungen zu Dialog 4.
	Bearbeiten Sie die zum Dialog gehörenden Übungen.
	Prägen Sie sich die *Wichtigen Wörter und Ausdrücke* ein.
	Arbeiten Sie die *Grammatik* durch und bearbeiten Sie die Übungen.
	Bearbeiten Sie die *Leseübungen*.
	Nun folgen die *Radioauszüge* mit den dazugehörigen *Übungen*.
	Sprechen Sie selbst.
	Hören Sie sich alle CD-Texte noch einmal ohne Buch an.

Lösungen

Dialog 1

Übung 1: a./T, b./F, c./T, d./T, e./T, f./F.

Übung 2: a. I particularly enjoy the wildlife programmes. b. I really liked David Attenborough's series on Life on Earth. c. I also like sport, especially football. d. I like the good photography and a nice flow of dialogue.

Dialog 2

Übung 4: classical music: c., f.; a schools quiz: b., e.; plays: a., d.

Übung 5: a. don't know, early morning, five days a week; b. Radio 3, at about 5 p. m., five days a week; c. don't know, early morning, don't know; d. Radio 4, weekends, don't know.

Dialog 3

Übung 7: a./2, b./1, c./3, d./2, e./3.

Übung 8: a. The Times; b. The Financial Times; c. The Guardian; d. The Daily Telegraph; e. Daily Mail; f. Daily Mirror; g. Daily Star; h. Daily Express; i. The Sun.

Dialog 4

Übung 10: a. delivered; b. normally; c. customers; d. throughout the; e. to judge; f. on order.

Übung 11: Folgende Stellen sollten unterstrichen sein: just after the shop opens ... the *Guardian* and the *Star* ... It is always predictable ... The shop only sells the national English newspapers.

Grammatik

Übung 1: a. stands; has suffered; b. am; have watched/ have been watching; c. live; have been; d. visit; has become.

Übung 2: a. are; b. is; c. are; d. is; e. are.

Leseübungen

Übung 1: b. News review, The Money Programme; c. Theatre Night: Thunder, Zandy's Bride; d. The Natural World; e. Contemporary Mozart, Harty goes to Venice, Music at Night.

Übung 2: a. Weil sie krank und deshalb ein Verkehrsrisiko sind; b. nein, auch für andere Verkehrsteilnehmer; c. einen Ärzteführer; d. das Sicherheitspersonal vom Pier zu Brighton; e. ein Junge; f. sie wurde ins Krankenhaus gebracht und musste über Nacht dort bleiben; g. um eine Ausstellung von Modefotos; h. David Bailey.

Radioübungen

Übung 1, Text

Chris Reilly: Now we look at this morning's papers. They all lead with the story of MI 5 spy Michael Bettany who was jailed at the Old Bailey yesterday for twenty-three years. *The Sun* claim an exclusive front-page interview with the spy's former girlfriend, West German Gabriele Proschnow. Even *The Times* and *The Guardian* have written leading articles on the man who tried unsuccessfully to sell British secrets to the Russians. The *Daily Mail* is continuing its now exhaustive story on South African runner Zola Budd. Yesterday (it) was a visit to her grandfather's home in East London, and today it's a look at her coach and trainer. Another story carried in most of the papers is the massacre of eight children and two women in a New York flat. They were shot while watching television, and the murders have been linked with Puerto Rican drug dealing.

Übung 1, Lösung: a./2, b./2, c./1, d./2, e./2.

Übung 2, Text

On to a lighter side of the news and a funny story in *The Sun*. Police are hunting a set of false teeth lost by a man who absentmindedly put them in his fish and chip paper after he'd finished eating. He then dumped them in an Exeter litter bin. And in the *Daily Mail* you can get an insight on how to tell if your best friend has had a facelift without telling you. Look for thick hooped ear-rings and permanently raised eyebrows.

Übung 2, Lösung: a. ja; b. er nahm es heraus, nachdem er Fisch und Pommes frites gegessen hatte, und warf das Papier samt Gebiss dann in eine Mülltonne. c. die Polizei; d. in der Daily Mail; e. auf Hautringe um die Ohren und ständig hochgezogene Brauen.

Übung 3, Text

Here's a special announcement to all telephone users. British Telecom regret that after five o'clock on Wednesday the 18th of April, the Telecom Brighton Sales Enquiry Line will be temporarily closed. If you have a sales enquiry, staff will be on hand as usual at the Telecom phone shop in Hannington's. This doesn't affect payment of telephone accounts.

Übung 3, Lösung: ... sales enquiry ... temporarily ... 5 o'clock ... 18th ... phone ... accounts.

9 It was a sell-out!

Wegweiser

	Dialog 1 Hören Sie sich den Dialog bei geschlossenem Buch an.
	Hören Sie sich den Dialog bei geöffnetem Buch an (wenn nötig, mehrmals).
	Studieren Sie die Vokabeln und Erklärungen.
	Bearbeiten Sie die zum Dialog gehörenden Übungen.
	Dialog 2 Hören Sie sich den Dialog bei geschlossenem Buch an.
	Hören Sie sich den Dialog bei geöffnetem Buch an (wenn nötig, mehrmals).
	Studieren Sie Vokabeln und Erklärungen zu Dialog 2.
	Bearbeiten Sie die zum Dialog gehörenden Übungen.
	Dialog 3 Hören Sie sich den Dialog bei geschlossenem Buch an.
	Hören Sie sich den Dialog bei geöffnetem Buch an (wenn nötig, mehrmals).
	Studieren Sie Vokabeln und Erklärungen zu Dialog 3.
	Bearbeiten Sie die zum Dialog gehörenden Übungen.
	Dialog 4 Hören Sie sich den Dialog bei geschlossenem Buch an.
	Hören Sie sich den Dialog bei geöffnetem Buch an (wenn nötig, mehrmals).
	Studieren Sie die Vokabeln und Erklärungen.
	Bearbeiten Sie die zum Dialog gehörenden Übungen.
	Prägen Sie sich die *Wichtigen Wörter und Ausdrücke* ein.
	Arbeiten Sie die *Grammatik* durch und bearbeiten Sie die Übungen.
	Bearbeiten Sie die *Leseübungen*.

	Nun folgt ein *Radioauszug* mit *Übung.*
	Sprechen Sie selbst.
	Hören Sie sich alle CD-Texte noch einmal ohne Buch an.

Lösungen

Dialog 1

Übung 1: a./2, b./2, c./1, d./3, e./3.

Übung 2: True: c., e., f.; False; a., b., d.

Dialog 2

Übung 4: a. Can you recommend a good disco? b. Where can I go to a theatre performance which isn't so expensive? c. Where's a cheap place to eat? d. Where can I go to a pub to listen to music?

Übung 5: a. ... plenty of ... very little; b. ... 50 per cent of ...; c. half an hour; d. ... an enormous variety ... e. ... don't charge at all.

Dialog 3

Übung 7: a. Antigua; b. Barbados; c. Guyana; d. Ireland; e. Barbados; f. Trinidad.

Übung 8: a./2, b./1, c./2, d./1, e./1.

Dialog 4

Übung 10: a. = stage; b. = actor; c. = performance; d. = sell-out; e. = audience.

Übung 11: ... experience ... French ... audience ... restive ... elements ... walked ... performance.

Grammatik

Übung 1: Reihenfolge: been, caught, wanted, spoken, known, let, bought, travelled, gone.

Übung 2: a. I was full. I had eaten well. b. He went home. He had worked enough. c. She was happy. She had finally got a new car. d. After he had broken his arm, he had to go to hospital.

Übung 3: ... came ... was ... had seen ... couldn't ... said ... remembered ... had met.

Leseübungen

Übung 1: a. CBGB & OMFUG; b. Ballroom; c. Algonquin Hotel; d. Eddie Condon's; e. Lone Star Café.

Übung 2: a. 1, 3, 4; b. 2, 4; c. 1, 3, 5; d. £2; e. £2.

Radioübung

Text

Sean Bolger: Blancmange are at the Dome on the 25th, Friday the 25th, that's this Friday, all tickets four pounds, and it starts at half-past seven. And on the drama front: "The Fire Raiser" is the titel of a play on at the Nightingale in Brighton, and it runs until Saturday the 28th of April. It'll cost you £2 to get in or £1.50 if you've got a UB 40 or you're a student; curtain up is at 8 o'clock each night except for Mondays, Sundays and on Good Friday. Spear of Destiny – they're on the Top Rank in Brighton on Wednesday the 2nd of May, and special guests are the Shellaley Sisters. Tickets are £4 on the door or £3.50 in advance. And finally, Katchagoogoo will be at the Crawley Leisure Centre on Thursday the 31st of May. It may seem a long time ahead but I'm sure that'll go very quickly. That starts at half past seven and tickets are £4.50, and they're available from the Leisure Centre and also HMV and Virgin in Brighton.

Lösung: b. *The Nightingale:* until 28th April, all tickets £2 (£1.50 UB 40/students), 8.00 p. m.; c. *Crawley Leisure Centre:* 31st May, all tickets £4.50, 7.30 p. m.; d. *Top Rank:* 2nd May, all tickets £4 (£3.50 in advance).

10 Nine to five

Wegweiser

	Dialog 1 Hören Sie sich den Dialog bei geschlossenem Buch an.
	Hören Sie sich den Dialog mehrmals bei geöffnetem Buch an.
	Studieren Sie die zum Dialog gehörenden Vokabeln und Erklärungen.
	Bearbeiten Sie die zum Dialog gehörenden Übungen.
	Dialog 2 Hören Sie sich den Dialog bei geschlossenem Buch an.
	Hören Sie sich den Dialog bei geöffnetem Buch an (wenn nötig, mehrmals).
	Studieren Sie Vokabeln und Erklärungen zu Dialog 2.
	Bearbeiten Sie die zum Dialog gehörenden Übungen.
	Dialog 3 Hören Sie sich den Dialog bei geschlossenem Buch an.
	Hören Sie sich den Dialog bei geöffnetem Buch an (wenn nötig, mehrmals).
	Studieren Sie Vokabeln und Erklärungen zu Dialog 3.
	Bearbeiten Sie die zum Dialog gehörenden Übungen.
	Dialog 4 Hören Sie sich den Dialog bei geschlossenem Buch an.
	Hören Sie sich den Dialog bei geöffnetem Buch an (wenn nötig, mehrmals).
	Studieren Sie die Vokabeln und Erläuterungen zu Dialog 4.
	Bearbeiten Sie die zum Dialog gehörenden Übungen.
	Prägen Sie sich die *Wichtigen Wörter und Ausdrücke* ein.
	Arbeiten Sie die *Grammatik* durch und bearbeiten Sie die Übungen.
	Bearbeiten Sie die *Leseübungen*.

	Nun folgen die *Radioauszüge* mit den dazugehörigen Übungen.
	Sprechen Sie selbst.
	Hören Sie sich alle CD-Texte noch einmal ohne Buch an.

Lösungen

Dialog 1

Übung 1: a. job; b. meals; c. hours; d. members of staff; e. work; f. people.

Übung 2: a./A; b./A; c./D; d./A; e./D; f./A; g./A.

Dialog 2

Übung 4: a. A lot of my day and week involves travelling to the properties. b. I make phonecalls as necessary. c. I often have business lunches. d. I usually end up writing letters.

Übung 5: 1. = e, 2. = a, 3. = f, 4. = b, 5. = c, 6. = d.

Dialog 3

Übung 7: ... painter and decorator ... self-employed ... responsible ... travel ... freedom ... lecturer ... security.

Übung 8: a./F, b./T, c./T, d./F, e./T, f./T.

Dialog 4

Übung 10: a. Saturdays and Sundays; b. a day's leave earned by working extra hours; c. accumulate; d. instead of; e. yearly holiday; f. a day's leave; g. with little warning.

Übung 11: (about) 26 ... 12 ... 35 ... 1.

Übung 12: a. CONDITIONS; b. OFF; c. MORNING; d. PHONE; e. ANNUAL; f. NATIONAL; g. YEAR= **COMPANY**.

Grammatik

Übung 1: a. A lot of wine is drunk in France. b. Jaguar cars are made in England. c. The new hotel will be finished soon. d. Exports from Japan to Europe have been increased.

Übung 2: a. Two ships were rescued by the Navy. b. New computers were (*oder* are) produced by Japanese companies. c. The moon was first reached by American astronauts. d. A new hospital was promised by the governor.

Leseübungen

Übung 1: About yourself: 1 = f., 2 = i., 3 = h., 4 = d., 5 = c.. About the job: 1 = a., 2 = g., 3 = e., 4 = b.

Übung 2: a. sales assistant; b. industrial painter; c. industrial painter; d. sales assistant.

Radioübungen

Übung 1, Text

Andrew Winter: All the jobs in this morning's job spot are in the Henfield area. A petrol station in the village needs a forecourt attendant aged over 25. You'll be working between half past seven and half past one or between half past one and half seven on alternate shifts; and there'll be some Sunday working too. The starting pay there is £70 a week.

Chris Copsey: A firm of contract gardeners in Henfield needs a gardener to work a 45 hour week. They'd like someone fully experienced in general and landscape gardening. It would be a help too if you have a clean driving licence. The job's open to any age group providing you have the experience to offer. And the pay, that's negotiable but likely to be around £90 a week. Those are just a selection of the jobs available in the Henfield area; if you're interested, Hove Job Centre have many more vacancies for that particular area. And the person to contact, that's Paula Dobson at Hove Job Centre. And Paula's on Brighton 410 266. That's Brighton 410 266.

Übung 1, Lösung: 1. Location: petrol station in Henfield village. Hours: 7.30–1.30/1.30–7.30. Pay: £70 per week. Special requirements: age over 25, some Sunday work. 2. Job description: gardener. Location: Henfield. Hours: 45 hours a week. Pay: £90. Special requirements: clean driving licence.

Übung 2, Text

Sue Taylor: Jobs are to be cut in the Planning Department at East Sussex County Council. Councillors have agreed to the cutback after hearing that some planning work no longer has to be done and that the administration is rather high. Council Leader John Chatfield says he hopes they'll find some other ways of losing staff apart from compulsory redundancy but he refuses to say exactly how many jobs will have to go.

John C.: The figure that I have in the back of my mind could vary either way by as many as ten. So I prefer not to give a figure, not least because of the concern of individuals in the department at the present time. Yes, there will be a reduction, there will be a perceptible reduction, but it will be one consistent with our continuing effectiveness and I believe improved effectiveness in all that we do.

Übung 2, Lösung: a./F, b./F, c./F, d./T, e./F, f./T, g./F, h./T.

11 How things are organized

Wegweiser

	Dialog 1 Hören Sie sich den Dialog bei geschlossenem Buch an.
	Hören Sie sich den Dialog bei geöffnetem Buch an (wenn nötig, mehrmals).
	Studieren Sie Vokabeln und Erklärungen zu Dialog 1.
	Bearbeiten Sie die zum Dialog gehörenden Übungen.
	Dialog 2 Hören Sie sich den Dialog bei geschlossenem Buch an.
	Hören Sie sich den Dialog bei geöffnetem Buch an (wenn nötig, mehrmals).
	Studieren Sie Vokabeln und Erklärungen zu Dialog 2.
	Bearbeiten Sie die zum Dialog gehörenden Übungen.
	Dialog 3 Hören Sie sich den Dialog bei geschlossenem Buch an.
	Hören Sie sich den Dialog bei geöffnetem Buch an (wenn nötig, mehrmals).

	Studieren Sie Vokabeln und Erklärungen zu Dialog 3.
	Bearbeiten Sie die zum Dialog gehörenden Übungen.
	Prägen Sie sich die *Wichtigen Wörter und Ausdrücke* ein.
	Bearbeiten Sie die *Leseübungen.*
	Arbeiten Sie die *Grammatik* durch und bearbeiten Sie die *Übungen.*
	Nun folgt ein *Radioauszug* mit dazugehöriger *Übung.*
	Sprechen Sie selbst.
	Hören Sie sich alle CD-Texte noch einmal ohne Buch an.

Lösungen

Dialog 1

Übung 1: Government 5, Cabinet 6, Opposition 2, Speaker 3, Civil Servants 4.

Übung 2: from ... slightly above ... in ... on your left ... on ... on your right ... in front of you ... Over ...

Dialog 2

Übung 4: a. = mountain rescue; b. = fire brigade; c. = coast guard; d. = ambulance; e. = police.

Übung 5: a. run by; b. responsibilities for; c. is organized ... controlled; d. under ... direct control.

Dialog 3

Übung 7: a. as a trainee teacher; b. as a teacher; c. as a teacher; d. as a teacher; e. as a pupil.

Übung 8: a./F, b./F, c./T, d./F, e./T.

Leseübungen

Übung 1: Commons, debate, bench, ministers.

Übung 2: a. seit 1957; b. dagegen; c. an Leo Amerys Worte; d. Oliver Cromwell; e. auf Urlaub fahren und am Strand herumplanschen; f. eine Ruhepause.

Übung 3: a. No; b. Yes; c. No; d. Yes; e. Yes; f. No; g. Yes.

Grammatik

Übung 1: a. He will mark your assignments. b. It will be sent through the post. c. You will have to study several hours per day. d. You will have plenty of time to choose the right one for you.

Übung 2: a. Er arbeitet zu hart – er macht sich noch krank. b. Da ist die Türklingel – ich geh' ran. c. Ich mag Joe – er hört einem immer zu. d. Was für ein kluger kleiner Junge – er wird bestimmt ein guter Schüler (werden).

Radioübungen

Übung 1, Text

Chris Reilly: Traders at George Street in Hove are rejoicing this evening because the Council's decided to scrap a car ban on Saturdays. Sue Maskell reports.

Sue Maskell: The experiment, which was on Saturdays only, began amid controversy. Traders said it would make them lose money and bitterly opposed the scheme. Now it's been ended prematurely but the chairman of the streets traders' association, Oscar Danin, says although he's pleased it's nothing to celebrate.

Oscar Danin: It's rather like having a serious operation. Now is a period for recuperation. We've got to get over it. I've already said I'm not too sure that the money can be got back, there's no way of recovering it quickly. But every effort will be made now to get as much back as possible, at least with the knowledge that the scheme isn't hanging over our heads.

Sue Maskell: The move has made Hove Councillor Bob Bailey furious. He also says that no-one's consulted the ratepayers who seem to have favoured the scheme.

Bob Bailey: Up to 90 per cent of ratepayers were in favour of the scheme. I'm a keen environmentalist, I like pedestrian schemes, whether I would have voted or not for the scheme at the end of the 6 month period I don't know but we should certainly have allowed the 6 month experiment to continue and then we should have looked at all the evidence, and as far as I know there is no evidence before the committee that the scheme is a great loser for the traders. Whether or not they've shown their books to the Council I don't know. I suspect not.

Sue Maskell: A survey of 68 George Street traders showed that only 3 were in favour of pedestrianisation.

Übung 1, Lösung: a./3, b./2, c./1, d./2, e./2, f./1.

12 Technology changes so quickly

Wegweiser

	Dialog 1 Hören Sie sich den Dialog bei geschlossenem Buch an.
	Hören Sie sich den Dialog mehrmals bei geöffnetem Buch an.
	Studieren Sie die Vokabeln und Erklärungen.
	Bearbeiten Sie die zum Dialog gehörenden Übungen.
	Dialog 2 Hören Sie sich den Dialog bei geschlossenem Buch an.
	Hören Sie sich den Dialog bei geöffnetem Buch an (wenn nötig, mehrmals).
	Studieren Sie Vokabeln und Erklärungen zu Dialog 2.
	Bearbeiten Sie die zum Dialog gehörenden Übungen.
	Dialog 3 Hören Sie sich den Dialog bei geschlossenem Buch an.
	Hören Sie sich den Dialog bei geöffnetem Buch an (wenn nötig, mehrmals).
	Studieren Sie Vokabeln und Erklärungen zu Dialog 3.

	Bearbeiten Sie die zum Dialog gehörenden Übungen.
	Prägen Sie sich die *Wichtigen Wörter und Ausdrücke* ein.
	Bearbeiten Sie die *Leseübungen*.
	Arbeiten Sie die *Grammatik* durch und bearbeiten Sie die *Übungen*.
	Nun folgen die *Radioauszüge* mit den dazugehörigen *Übungen*.
	Sprechen Sie selbst.
	Hören Sie sich alle CD-Texte noch einmal ohne Buch an.

Lösungen

Dialog 1

Übung 1: a. A; b. TV; c. SET; d. HAIR; e. DRYER; f. WASHER; g. FREEZER; h. ENLARGER; i. COFFEE POT; j. TYPEWRITER; k. THE DARKROOM; l. REFRIGERATOR; m. ELECTRIC CLOCK; n. A HUNDRED AND TEN.

Übung 2: a. typewriter, hair dryer; b. radio, vacuum cleaner; c. coffee pot, toaster, tumble dryer.

Dialog 2

Übung 4: b./III, c./I, d./V, e./II, f./VII, g./IV.

Übung 5: True: b., d., e. False: a., c.

Dialog 3

Übung 7: a. Yes, he would. b. No, he hasn't. c. No, he doesn't. d. Yes, he would. e. Yes, he did. f. Yes, he would.

Übung 8: b. Chris would buy himself a new dishwashing unit. c. Doris would buy herself a stereo set. d. Mark would buy himself a video recorder. e. Francis would buy himself a sailing yacht. f. Catherine would buy herself an electric typewriter.

Leseübungen

Übung 1: a. = Photo copiers; b. = House phones; c. = Computers; d. = Video.

Übung 2: a. das Videogerät; b. die Telefone; c. die Telefone; d. Toshiba; e. ein Fotokopiergerät.

Grammatik

Übung 1: a. Swimming in the sea is wonderful. b. I heard his loud singing. c. She is proud of looking like a film star. d. He succeeded in getting there first. e. We are used to getting up early.

Übung 2: a. Möchten Sie zur Party kommen? b. Möchten Sie, dass ich zur Party komme? c. Ich mag keine Zigarren (rauchen). d. Ich mag es nicht, wenn mein Vater Zigarren raucht. e. Es besteht keine Hoffnung, das Flugzeug zu erreichen. f. Es besteht keine Hoffnung für die Passagiere, das Flugzeug zu erreichen.

Radioübungen

Übung 1 und 2, Text

David Howells: The most advanced body scanner in the country is about to be delivered to the Royal Sussex County Hospital in Brighton. The new machine will replace one which is seven years old. Richard Phillips reports.

Richard Phillips: At a cost of just under half a million pounds the scanner will go into the Charles Honeysett Unit. It was Mr Honeysett who bought the machine it replaces and his family have provided a quarter of a million towards the new machinery. The rest has come from Brighton Health Authority and the authority of the South East Thames region.

The makers of the scanner describe it as the most comprehensive and sophisticated in the world; it'll be used to diagnose spinal problems, head injuries, and to trace cancers. The new machine is expected to be fully operational at the Royal Sussex County Hospital in the middle of June.

Übung 1 und 2, Lösung: a. BODY; b. SCANNER; c. HONEYSETT; d. REPLACE; e. FAMILY; f. TRACE; g. CANCERS; h. SOPHISTICATED; i. DIAGNOSE; j. PROBLEMS = BENEFACTOR.

Übung 3, Text

Chris Reilly: Southdown Bus Company have won an award for the use of a computer to help cut costs. Accountant Rosemary Holland, who works for South Down, explains what the micro-computer does and how it saves the bus company money.

Rosemary Holland: About two years ago we won an award issued by the Chairman of the National Bus company, for the micro-computer system for producing fare tables. Where previously we had paid a considerable amount of money each time to produce the fare table, on art work, we use a simple programme to update fares as and when there are fares increases and then produce a revised print of each fare table for each service. That is then photocopied and issued to all of the drivers.
Previously we had to use printers. We found that the initial cost of the computer system was more than covered during the first year by the savings in payments we would have previously made.

Übung 3, Lösung: a./T, b./F, c./F, d./T, e./T, f./F.